Heart and Lungs

Andrew Solway

W

FRANKLIN WATTS

LONDON•SYDNEY

Franklin Watts
338 Euston Road
London NW1 3BH

Franklin Watts Australia
Level 17/207 Kent Street
Sydney NSW 2000

Series editor: Sarah Peutrill
Art director: Jonathan Hair
Design: Mo Choy
Photographer: Paul Bricknell, unless otherwise stated
Illustations: Ian Thompson
Consultant: Peter Riley

With thanks to our models: Celine Clark, Chay Harrison,
Akash Kohli, Liam Lane, Kate Polley and Eoin Serle.

Picture credits: Andy Crawford: 3, 4, 13, 16, 19b, 24, 26,
27. Michael Donne/SPL: 29. Image Source/Corbis: 11.
Inner Space Imaging/SPL: 17. Kimimasa
Mayama/Reuters/Corbis: 27. NASA: 13.
Alain Pol, ISM/SPL: 25.

A CIP catalogue record for this book is available from
the British Library.

Dewey number: 612.1
ISBN: 978 1 4451 3881 7

Printed in China

Franklin Watts is a division of Hachette Children's Books,
an Hachette UK company.
www.hachette.co.uk

Contents

The heart and lungs

If you can, run on the spot. Keep going for a couple of minutes. Then do some jumping on the spot.

Do you feel tired? How is your breathing? If you have been working hard, you will be breathing faster.

Put both hands on the front of your chest. Can you feel something thumping? That is your heart beating.

When you notice your breathing, and feel your heart thumping, you are feeling your heart and lungs at work.

When you run and jump, ▶ your heart beats faster. Your breathing gets faster and deeper, too.

Inside your chest

Your heart and lungs are inside your chest. You have two lungs. The heart is between them. But what do they do? Why does your heart beat? Why do you breathe? And why does your heart thump harder when you exercise? Read on to find out all about the heart and lungs.

◀ *Your heart and lungs are in your chest. The heart is slightly over to the left; because of this the left lung is smaller than the right.*

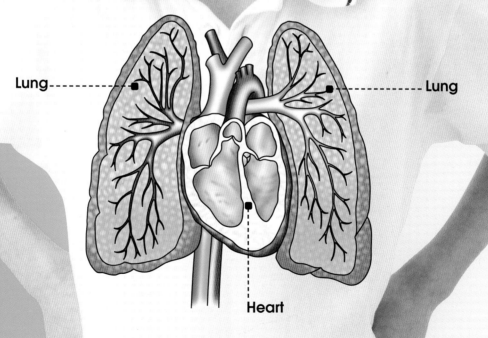

Lung - Lung

Heart

Billions of heartbeats

Your heart beats about 2.5 billion times during your lifetime.
You breathe in and out a lot too – about 550 million times.

The heart is a muscle

Bend your arm up. Feel the top muscle. It will feel hard and fat. Now relax your arm. Feel the muscle again. It feels softer, and thin.

Contracting and relaxing

When a muscle works, it contracts. This means it gets shorter and fatter. When the muscle stops working, it relaxes. The muscle gets longer and thinner.

▲
When you bend your arm, the biceps muscle contracts. When you straighten your arm it relaxes.

Biceps

Elbow joint

Skeletal muscle

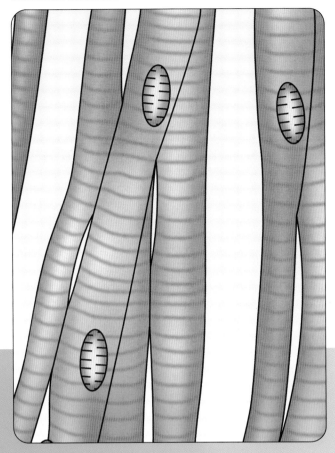

Cardiac muscle

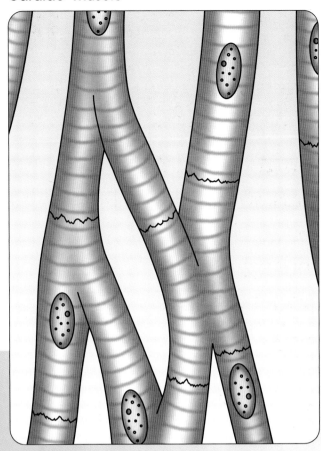

▲

When heart muscle is magnified, you can see that the muscle fibres branch and connect with each other. Other muscle is not like this.

Cardiac muscle

The heart is also a muscle. It contracts and relaxes with every heartbeat. However, the heart is a very special type of muscle, called cardiac muscle. Other muscles get tired when they have been working for a while. The heart does not get tired. It keeps beating without stopping all your life, until you die.

Try this!

Jump from one foot to the other for as long as you can. How long before your legs feel tired? You probably get tired after just a few minutes. This shows how different your heart muscles are from your leg muscles. Your heart muscle never gets tired.

The heart is a pump

The heart is a muscular pump. Inside the heart there are four spaces, called chambers. The heart pumps blood in and out of these chambers.

Blood in and out

When the muscles around a chamber relax, the chamber gets bigger, and blood flows in. When the muscles contract, they push blood out of the chamber.

The heart has four ▶ chambers. There are two ventricles (the left ventricle and the right ventricle) and two atria (the left atrium and the right atrium).

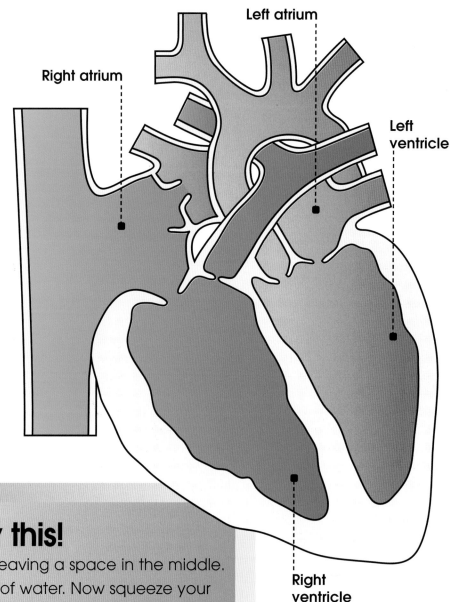

Left atrium

Right atrium

Left ventricle

Right ventricle

Try this!

Put your hands together, leaving a space in the middle. Put your hands in a sink of water. Now squeeze your hands together, so that water squirts out. This is similar to the way the heart squeezes blood out of the chambers.

Valves

Valves in the heart make sure blood flows through the heart in a certain direction. A valve lets liquid flow one way, but not the other. The heart valves are flaps, rather like doors. When blood flows in one direction, it pushes the valve 'doors' open. When blood tries to flow the other way, the 'doors' are pushed closed.

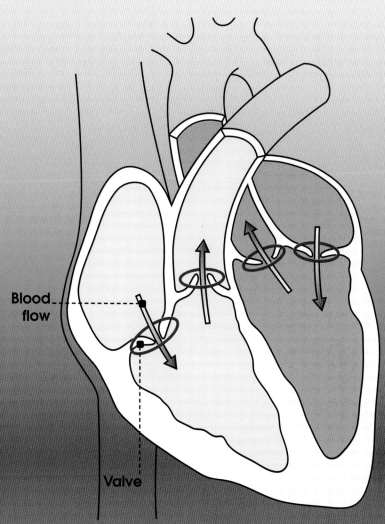

Blood flow

Valve

◀ *Valves control the flow of blood into and out of the heart chambers. In this picture the four heart valves are circled.*

When you pump up a bicycle ▶ tyre, you push air out of the pump and into the tyre. A valve stops the air escaping again. The heart has valves too, but the heart's valves (and its walls) stop blood escaping rather than air.

9

What is blood for?

The heart pumps blood all round the body. The blood travels through tubes called blood vessels. Blood vessels that carry blood away from the heart are called arteries. Vessels that carry blood back to the heart are called veins.

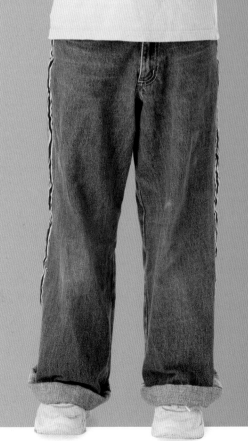

Carrying oxygen
Blood does several important jobs. First of all, it contains billions of tiny cells. Most of these are red blood cells. Their job is to carry oxygen all round the body. The oxygen comes from your lungs.

Carrying energy
Blood also carries the goodness from food. All the cells in the body need energy to work. They get their energy from a sugar called glucose. Glucose is carried to all parts of the body in the blood.

Keeping well

Finally, blood also helps to defend the body from harm. When you get a cut, blood clots (goes thick) in the wound. Soon the blood forms a hard scab that keeps germs out of the wound. There are also special cells in the blood, called white blood cells, that get rid of any germs that actually get into the body.

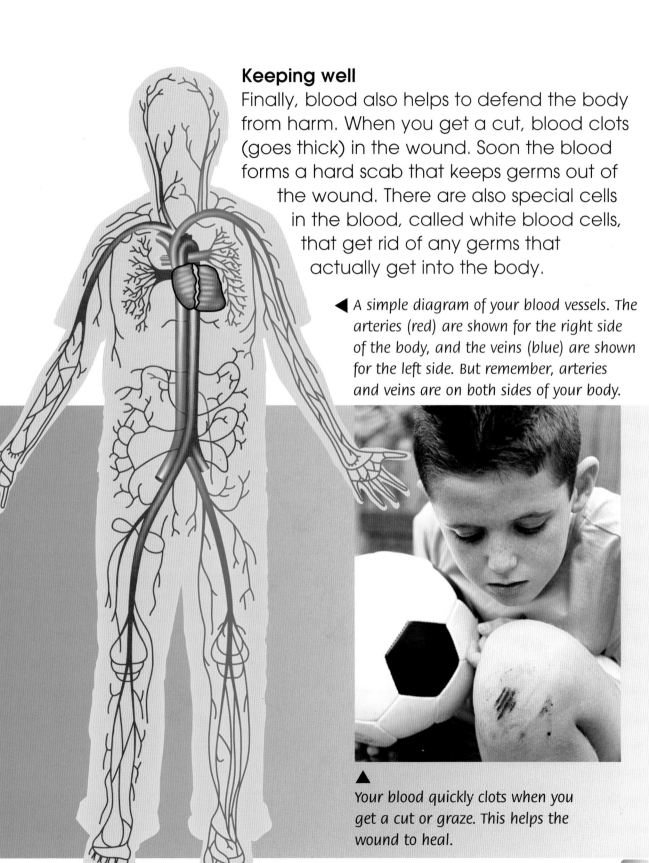

◀ *A simple diagram of your blood vessels. The arteries (red) are shown for the right side of the body, and the veins (blue) are shown for the left side. But remember, arteries and veins are on both sides of your body.*

▲
Your blood quickly clots when you get a cut or graze. This helps the wound to heal.

We need oxygen

Oxygen is a gas that is found in the air. When we breathe in, we take in oxygen. It goes into our lungs, and from there it goes into the blood.

We breathe in air through our nose and mouth. The air goes down a tube called the windpipe and into the lungs.
▼

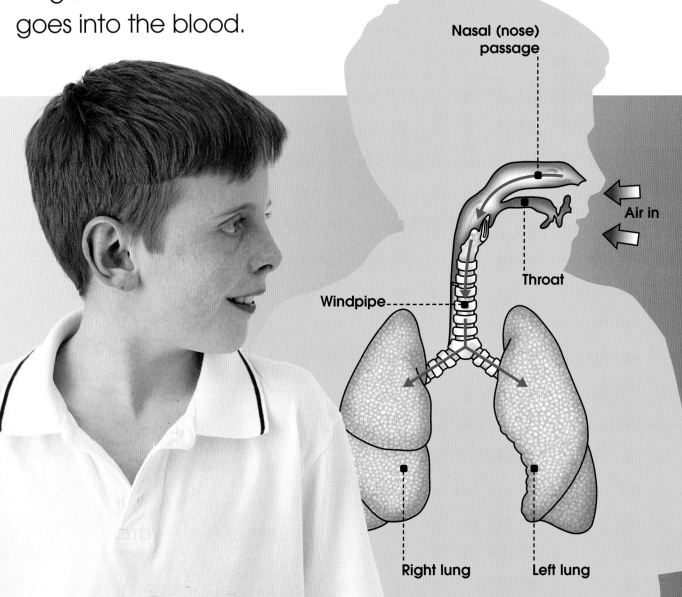

Nasal (nose) passage

Air in

Throat

Windpipe

Right lung

Left lung

Oxygen tanks

We cannot breathe under water or out in space. Divers and astronauts have to carry a supply of oxygen in tanks on their back.

Oxygen gives us energy

Our bodies need energy all the time. We use it to move and to grow. Even when we are asleep we need energy. We get energy from our food, which is the body's fuel. However, we also need oxygen. Your body uses the oxygen to burn up the fuel, and this gives us energy.

When we are active, ▶ playing games or sports, we use more energy than when we sit still.

Your ribs move

In…out…in…out. Breathing is like your heartbeat. It goes on all your life. When you breathe in, your ribs move out and up. Your stomach moves out, too.

Breathing in

The stomach moves because of a muscle called the diaphragm. This stretches across the bottom of the ribs. As you breathe in, the diaphragm contracts and pulls the bottom of the lungs down and pushes the tummy area out.

Try this!

Put your hands on your ribs. Now breathe in and out. Try the same thing with your hands on your stomach. Feel how your ribs and stomach move.

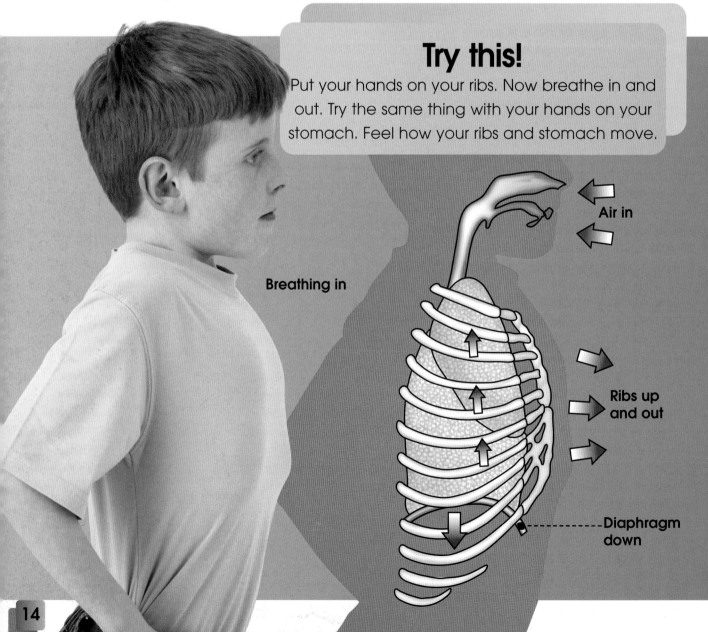

Breathing in

Air in

Ribs up and out

Diaphragm down

Breathing out

As you breathe out, the diaphragm relaxes. The ribs move down and in.

Bigger and smaller

The movements of the ribs and the diaphragm change the size of the lungs. As you breathe in the lungs expand (grow bigger). Air is sucked into them. As you breathe out the lungs contract (shrink). This pushes air out of them.

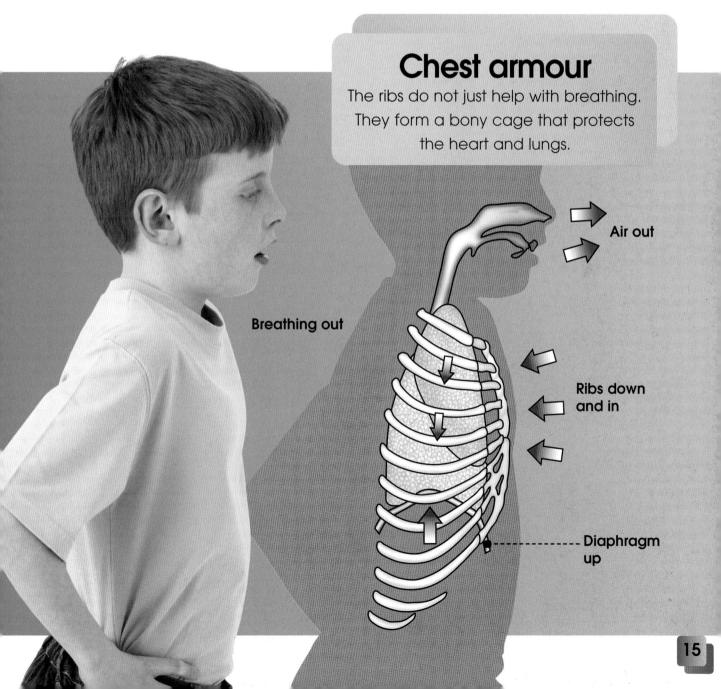

Chest armour

The ribs do not just help with breathing. They form a bony cage that protects the heart and lungs.

Breathing out

Air out

Ribs down and in

Diaphragm up

Lungs are sponges

It's easy to think that the lungs are like two balloons. Actually, they are more like sponges. Your lungs are two fleshy, stretchy sacks filled with tiny air tubes.

A sponge has lots of air spaces inside it. When you put the sponge in water, the water fills these spaces. Your lungs can fill up with air in the same way. They have lots of tiny air tubes. When you breathe in, air fills these tubes.

Bronchus

A tube called a bronchus (called bronchi when you're talking about more than one) brings air to each lung. This tube then splits up into smaller and smaller air tubes called bronchioles. The smallest tubes are so tiny that they are microscopic. Each tube ends in tiny air sacs called alveoli. They are like tiny pockets of air.

This X-ray shows the air ▶ tubes inside the lungs. The large bronchi branch many times to form millions of tiny tubes.

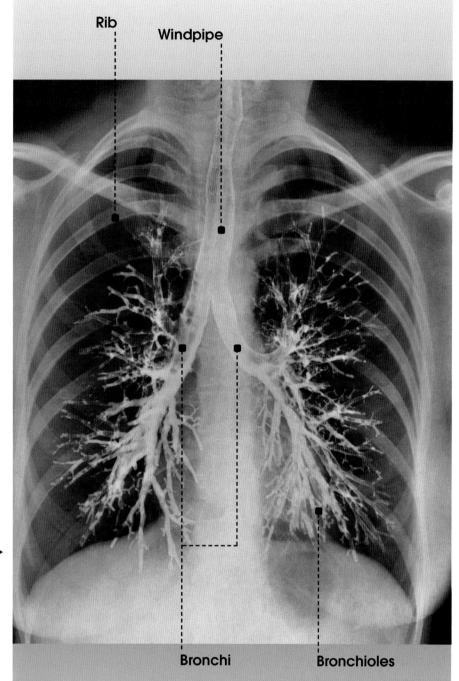

Rib

Windpipe

Bronchi

Bronchioles

Billions of tubes

If you could lay out the air tubes in your lungs end to end, they would stretch 2,400 kilometres. That's the distance from London to Madrid, in Spain, and back again!

Gases in and out

Why are there so many tiny tubes in the lungs? It is so that the air in the lungs can get close to the blood.

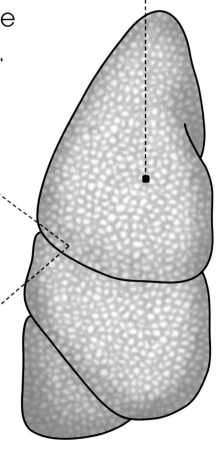

Lung

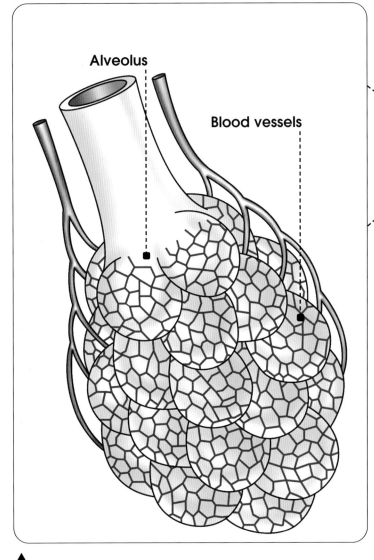

Alveolus

Blood vessels

▲
Our lungs contain about 300 million alveoli. Each one is surrounded by a network of blood vessels.

Air sacs
Each air sac – called an alveolus – is surrounded by a net of very small blood vessels. It is easy for oxygen to move from these air sacs (alveoli) into the blood.

Waste gas

When your body uses oxygen to make energy, another gas, carbon dioxide, is a waste product. The blood carries carbon dioxide back to the lungs. At the same time as oxygen goes into the blood, carbon dioxide moves from the blood to the alveoli.

So when you breathe in, your lungs take in fresh oxygen. And when you breathe out, you get rid of waste carbon dioxide.

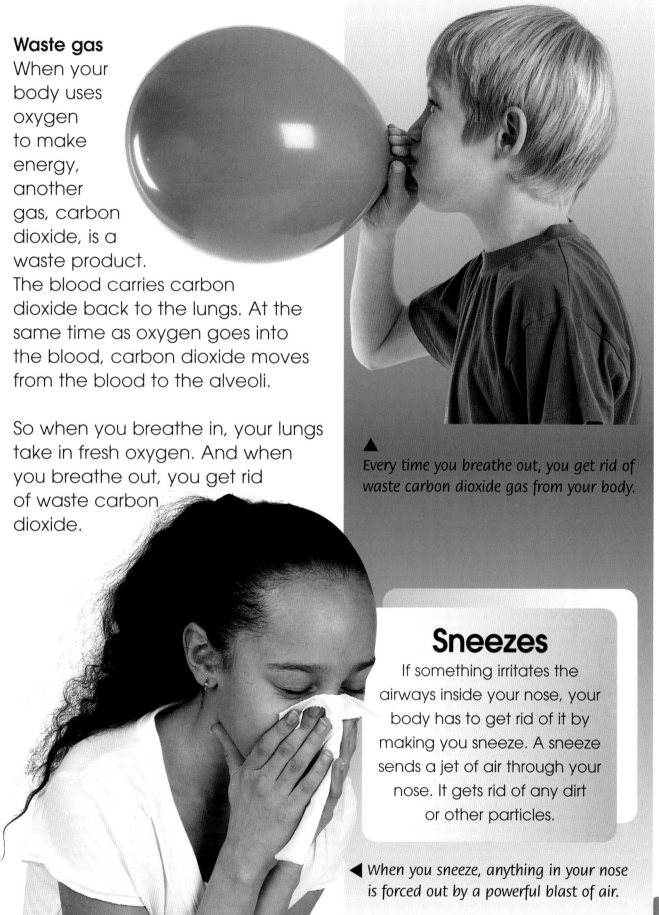

▲ Every time you breathe out, you get rid of waste carbon dioxide gas from your body.

Sneezes

If something irritates the airways inside your nose, your body has to get rid of it by making you sneeze. A sneeze sends a jet of air through your nose. It gets rid of any dirt or other particles.

◀ When you sneeze, anything in your nose is forced out by a powerful blast of air.

The blood system

When your blood has collected oxygen and removed carbon dioxide from your lungs, it then goes to your heart.

Around the body

The heart pumps blood around the body. As the blood travels through the body's blood vessels, it gradually gives up its oxygen to the body's cells. At the same time, the cells release waste carbon dioxide into the blood.

Long piping

If you laid all the blood vessels in your body end to end, they would stretch 9,700 kilometres – about the distance from London to Tokyo in Japan.

All the main organs of the body, such as the liver and the heart, have a network of blood vessels that bring them food and oxygen.
▼

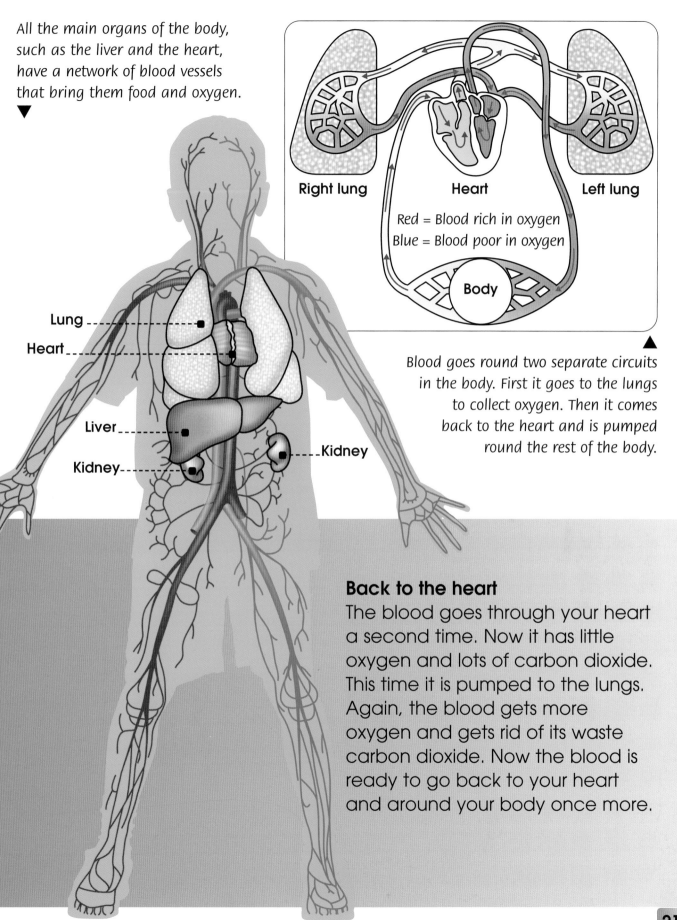

Right lung   Heart   Left lung

Red = Blood rich in oxygen
Blue = Blood poor in oxygen

Body

Lung

Heart

Liver

Kidney

Kidney

▲

Blood goes round two separate circuits in the body. First it goes to the lungs to collect oxygen. Then it comes back to the heart and is pumped round the rest of the body.

Back to the heart

The blood goes through your heart a second time. Now it has little oxygen and lots of carbon dioxide. This time it is pumped to the lungs. Again, the blood gets more oxygen and gets rid of its waste carbon dioxide. Now the blood is ready to go back to your heart and around your body once more.

The four-part heart

The heart is not one pump, it is two. Each of the heart's two pumps has two chambers: an atrium and a ventricle.

▲ *Doctors use a stethoscope to listen to the sound of the heartbeat.*

Two pumps

The right side of the heart pumps blood to the lungs and back. The left side pumps blood to the rest of the body when it comes back from the lungs. Both sides pump at the same time.

The diagram opposite shows how blood is pumped through the heart.

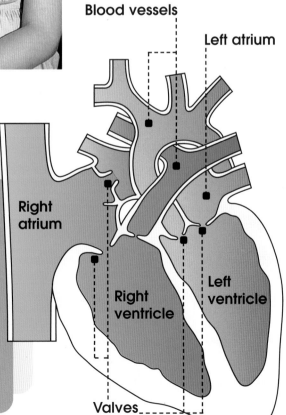

Blood vessels

Left atrium

Right atrium

Right ventricle

Left ventricle

Valves

Lub-dub, lub-dub

Do you know what your heart sounds like? It has a double beat – lub-dub, lub-dub. The sounds are made by the heart valves. The first sound is one set of heart valves slamming shut as the ventricles contract. The second sound is another set of valves shutting as blood rushes back into the heart.

1
- The right atrium fills up with oxygen-poor blood.
- The atrium contracts. This squeezes the blood into the right ventricle.

2
Now the right ventricle contracts. Whoosh! The blood shoots out of the heart and into the blood vessels. The blood goes to the lungs.

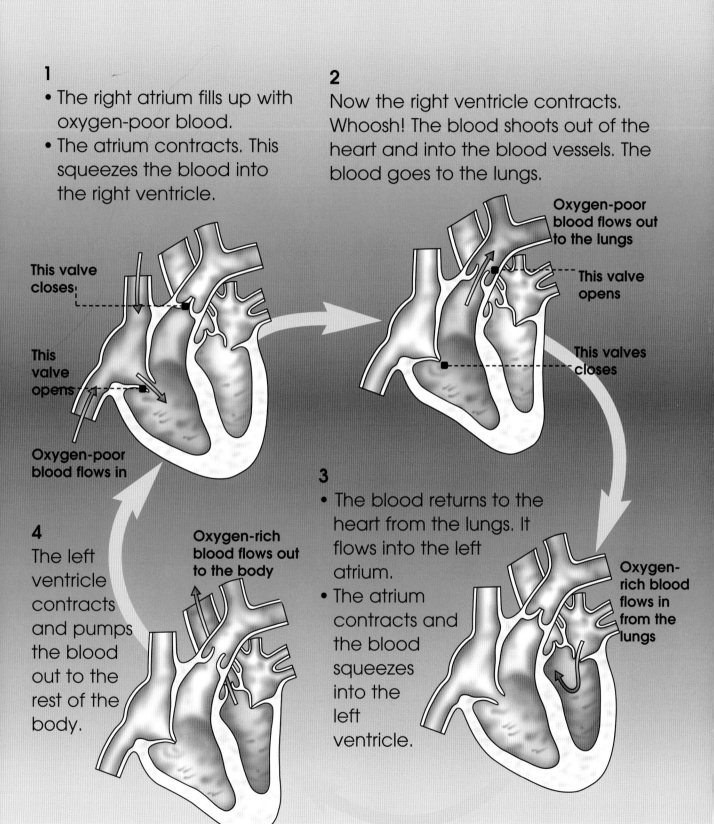

This valve closes

This valve opens

Oxygen-poor blood flows in

Oxygen-poor blood flows out to the lungs

This valve opens

This valves closes

4
The left ventricle contracts and pumps the blood out to the rest of the body.

Oxygen-rich blood flows out to the body

3
- The blood returns to the heart from the lungs. It flows into the left atrium.
- The atrium contracts and the blood squeezes into the left ventricle.

Oxygen-rich blood flows in from the lungs

A healthy heart

Most of us are born with a healthy heart. It is important to keep it healthy. It has to last a lifetime! One way of making sure your heart stays healthy is to eat well. What we eat can affect the heart.

Keep a balance

To keep the heart healthy, eat a balanced diet. This means eating at least five servings of fresh fruit and vegetables a day, and not eating too many sweets or fatty foods.

Fruit is good for you ▶ because it contains lots of vitamins and minerals. It tastes good too!

Fatty and salty

Fats can coat the inside of blood vessels. Sometimes a blood vessel can become completely blocked. This is why it is not good to eat too many fatty foods. Too much salt is also bad for the heart.

Fruit and vegetables

Meat, eggs, fish and pulses, such as lentils and beans

Fatty and sugary foods, such as crisps, sweets and fizzy drinks

Bread, cereals, potatoes, rice, noodles

Milk, cheese, yoghurt

▲

This is a way to check you are getting a balanced diet. You should eat more of the things that have a large slice of the plate, such as bread and fruit. You should eat less of the things with a smaller slice of the plate.

▲

This X-ray shows someone with heart disease. The shadowy dark orange area is the heart, which has enlarged and is squashing the lungs (blue).

No smoking!

If you want a healthy heart and lungs, then don't smoke! Chemicals in cigarette smoke make your heart beat faster. Over a long period, this strains the heart. Tar in the smoke coats the inside of the lungs. This makes your lungs work less well and may cause cancer and other diseases.

Strong heart and lungs

Exercise is also good for the heart and lungs. Running, swimming, skipping, cycling and all kinds of sports are good ways to exercise.

◀ Skipping is fun, and good exercise too. Boxers, for example, do lots of skipping to get fit and speed up their footwork.

How does exercise help?

The heart is a muscle and all muscles need to 'work out' to keep them in the best condition. When you exercise, you use more energy. If you use more energy you need more oxygen. You breathe more quickly, to get more air into your lungs.

Your heart pumps faster and harder, to move the blood round the body more quickly. So when you exercise, your heart and lungs exercise too. This helps to keep them healthy. Getting puffed out is good for you!

Big-hearted

A normal person has a resting heart rate of around 80 beats per minute. Top long-distance runners have bigger, stronger hearts. Their hearts can pump more blood with each beat. This means they beat more slowly. A long distance runner's heart beats more slowly than the hearts of other people. Athletes have bigger lungs, too.

Top endurance athletes like Paula Radcliffe have a very strong heart and large lungs.
▼

Checking your pulse

Hold one hand palm up. Rest the first two fingers of the other hand gently on the upper part of your wrist. Can you feel a gentle, regular movement? This is your pulse. It is a way of feeling your heartbeat.

Resting rate

Sit calm and relaxed. How many beats of your pulse can you feel in 15 seconds? Multiply the answer by four. This is your resting heart rate.

Working rate

Now do two minutes of hard exercise such as running. Are you out of breath? Take your pulse again. This is your working heart rate.

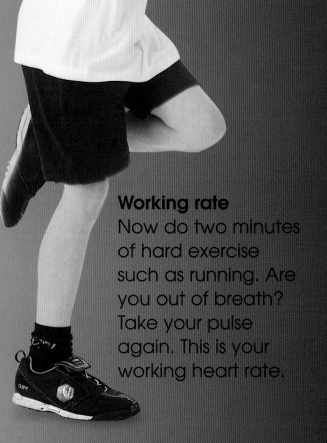

The heart at work

You will find that your pulse is faster after exercise. Your breathing will be quicker and deeper, too. Now you have read this book, you can understand why this happens. When you exercise, your body uses more energy. This means it needs more oxygen. The changes in breathing and heart rate help you get more oxygen to your body's cells.

Heart monitor

Athletes regularly check their heart rate to see how their training is working. A slower heart rate usually means they are getting fitter. Many athletes use a special heart monitor to count their heartbeats, rather than taking their pulse.

The electrodes stuck to this man's body track changes in his heart rate as he exercises.

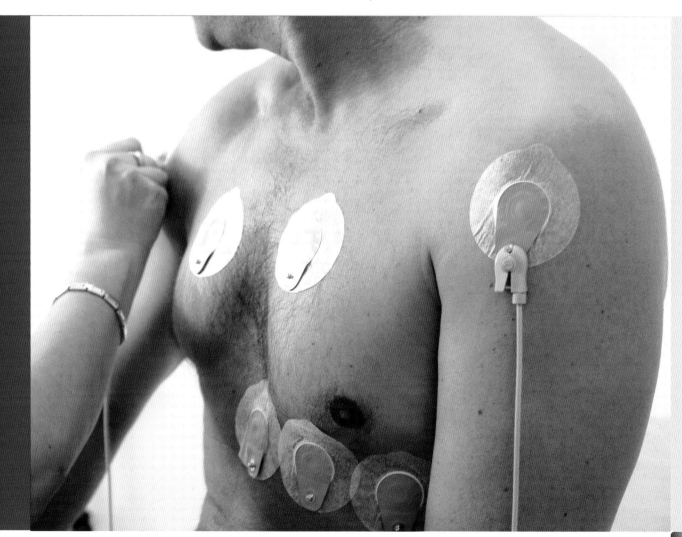

Glossary

alveolus (plural alveoli)
One of millions of tiny air spaces in the lungs, which are at the ends of the air tubes.

artery
A blood vessel that carries blood out from the heart to other parts of the body.

atrium (plural atria)
One of two chambers (spaces) inside the heart, where blood collects as it comes into the heart.

blood vessel
A tube that carries blood around the body.

bronchus (plural bronchi)
One of the main air tubes in the lungs.

cancer
A serious disease that causes lumps to grow in the body.

carbon dioxide
A gas that our bodies produce as waste. We get rid of carbon dioxide when we breathe out.

clotting
When blood is exposed to the air, it thickens and eventually goes solid. This is clotting.

contract
To get shorter.

diaphragm
A sheet of muscle underneath the lungs that moves up and down during breathing.

heart
The organ that pumps blood all around the body. It is made of a special muscle that never gets tired.

lungs
The organs you use to breathe. The lungs take in fresh air and push stale air out.

microscopic
Too small to be seen with your eye, but visible with an instrument called a microscope.

minerals
Very simple substances, such as calcium and iron, that we need to eat in small amounts to keep healthy.

muscle

The parts of the body that you use to move. Muscles work by contracting (getting shorter).

oxygen

A gas in the air, which humans and other animals need to keep them alive.

pulse

The regular beat of the heart, which can be felt at certain places, such as the wrist or the neck.

valve

In the heart, valves allow blood to flow one way but not the other.

vein

A blood vessel that brings blood back to the heart from other parts of the body.

ventricle

One of two chambers (spaces) inside the heart that have strong, muscular walls. The ventricles pump blood around the body.

vitamins

Substances that we get in our food, which we need to eat in small amounts to keep us healthy.

FURTHER INFORMATION
WEBSITES

www.bbc.co.uk/science/ humanbody/body
This website gives you games and interactive information about the human body.

www.kidshealth.org
Kidshealth gives you information about your body. Click on the section called 'for kids'.

Note to parents and teachers: Every effort has been made by the Publishers to ensure that these websites are suitable for children, that they are of the highest educational value, and that they contain no inappropriate or offensive material. However, because of the nature of the Internet, it is impossible to guarantee that the contents of these sites will not be altered. We strongly advise that Internet access is supervised by a responsible adult.

Index